Pietro Maria Ferré

Saint Thomas of Aquin and Ideology

A Discourse Read to the Accademia Roman

Pietro Maria Ferré

Saint Thomas of Aquin and Ideology
A Discourse Read to the Accademia Roman

ISBN/EAN: 9783744673495

Printed in Europe, USA, Canada, Australia, Japan

Cover: Foto ©ninafisch / pixelio.de

More available books at **www.hansebooks.com**

Saint Thomas of Aquin

AND

Ideology.

A Discourse read to the Accademia Romana,
18th August, 1870,

By MONSIGNOR FERRÉ,

BISHOP OF CASAL MONFERRATO, PIEDMONT.

Translated by a Father of Charity.

LONDON :

BURNS, OATES, AND CO., 17 AND 18, PORTMAN STREET, W.
1875.

PREFACE OF THE TRANSLATOR.

—::—

Half a century ago Rosmini wrote the following words :
" If Philosophy is to be restored to love and respect, I
" think it will be necessary, in part, to return to the
" teachings of the ancients, and in part, to give those teach-
" ings the benefit of modern methods, facility of style, a
" breadth of application embracing the daily wants of human
" life, and finally, to cement all the parts into one complete
" whole. The Schoolmen, now made so little of, are the
" link connecting the old with the modern philosophies, and
" deserve to be carefully studied. For, though the scho-
" lastic philosophy in its later period became degraded,
" childish, and ridiculous, it was not so in its great writers,
" among whom suffice it to mention the prince of Italian
" philosophers, S. Thomas of Aquin." *(Rosmini, Teodicea,*
n. 148.*)*

So wrote a great and holy man, grieved to the heart as
he ' beheld the havoc caused by modern philosophy—I
mean those systems which, having started from the
" sensation and reflection " principle òf Locke, have
grown successively into the more subtle, deep, and

insidious forms of *Subjectivism* whereof the Kantian theory is the centre.

Rosmini's voice has been re-echoed far and wide; and now the necessity of going back to the old teachings, so profoundly and so luminously expounded by the Angelic Doctor, is felt very generally among Catholic thinkers.

That honest and to some extent successful efforts have been made in that direction, is shown by some of the philosophical treatises now in circulation. It is very pleasing to observe in them so much that is really true and beautiful. Nevertheless, when we come to that most fundamental question—the "*origin of uni-*" "*versals*" or of human ideas, not one of those treatises gives a satisfactory reply, so far as is known to the writer of these lines. Some pass over the question altogether; others try to explain " universals " by means of an undefined sort of faculty natural to us, but not naturally informed with that *light* which is evidence itself; while others fall back upon the theory which pretends to form universal ideas by abstracting them from particular ones—an evident begging of the question. For, if our mind, observing the universal in the particular, abstracts it therefrom, clearly the universal is there already; else the mind could not observe it. So the question returns: " How " did the universal come there ?"

Now this seems like building a house of many storeys well and carefully arranged but without a foundation; or like constructing a locomotive without wheel or steam power. A main portion of the value of such books is wanting. So long as this continues, it will not be possible to establish effectually the essential objectivity and the unassailable certitude of human knowledge. Consequently it will not be possible to raise on a firm basis the moral sciences, and indeed any science whatever, natural or supernatural; for sciences are mere phantoms if their objectivity be not placed beyond the possibility of attack. The shrewd subjectivist will go on still smiling at good intentions not substantiated by valid deeds.

In the following Essay on " *Saint Thomas of Aquin and* " *Ideology*," from the pen of the highly-gifted, learned and painstaking Bishop of Casale, in Piedmont, an attentive reader will find a genuine sketch of the doctrine of S. Thomas upon two questions, a full answer to which would, as may be easily perceived, fill up the gap complained of. They are : 1st, " What is that light of reason whence we " derive the power of acquiring knowledge ?" 2nd, "By what " process does our mind pass from being simply informed " by the original light of reason to being possessed of " special cognitions ?"

Those who wish to see these two questions treated much more fully, as also a number of other questions more or less related to them, will find what they want in Rosmini's " *Nuovo Saggio sull' Origine delle Idee.*" This great ideological work in three volumes may be called the key to the whole of that vast system—universal and yet one—which has been developed in. a great variety of writings by the same author.*

THE TRANSLATOR.

* Translations of Rosmini's "*Nuovo Saggio*" and "*Teodicea*" are now in preparation for the press.

S. THOMAS OF AQUIN AND IDEOLOGY.

Illustrious Members of the Academia,—

1. While duly grateful for the high honour you have conferred on me by inviting me to address you on this occasion, I fear that I have accepted a responsibility heavier than I may be able to discharge in a fitting manner. What comforts me, however, is the reflection that, should I be found wanting, your well-known kindness will condescend to accept my good will for the deed.

2. In your former sittings of this year, the falsehoods and blasphemies of Pseudo-Janus were refuted by orators as learned as they were eloquent. With irresistible arguments they proved the Sovereign prerogative of the Primacy of S. Peter's Chair. They demonstrated by a long series of historical facts, that the Sovereign Pontiffs deserve to be called the champions of true progress— religious, moral, and civil—the promoters of justice, charity, science, and the benefactors and perfecters of human society. Likewise, they showed you with what care the Popes have always striven to respect those relations which God has ordained between the ecclesiastical and secular powers ; with what unswerving fidelity they have ever preserved divine truth, by defining the most difficult questions of faith and morality ; and, finally, how

unceasing have been their efforts to soften the rigours of justice with the mildness of clemency, and to foster as well as protect every manifestation of true and honest liberty.

It would seem that, as a fitting climax to all these truly precious disquisitions, I should now expatiate on the infallible teaching authority divinely conferred on the Visible Head of the Catholic Church. But so much has been said and written during this very year upon this grand theme, that it appears almost impossible to add anything. Moreover, the Holy Vatican Council now sitting has put the last seal to the entire question by its solemn definition—given in response to the ardent wishes of the Catholic world—and has thus supplied a very great and long-felt want of the Church.

3. But good and thoughtful men, while rejoicing in the new security and bulwark of defence thus provided for the unity of the faith, cannot but desire that a unity of sound principles should be established also as regards Philosophy —at least in all the Catholic Schools. For this end they would like to see the philosophical doctrines of the Fathers of the Church, but especially of S. Thomas of Aquin, restored to their ancient seat of honour. The truth of these doctrines cannot be doubted. It has been recognised by men who to great power of intellect and vast erudition added sublime sanctity.

Our security is still further increased by the fact that these doctrines are in perfect harmony with the teachings of Divine revelation. Therefore, this desire is as praiseworthy as the way of carrying it into effect is clear. But alas! instead of unaminity, we are doomed to witness a sad spectacle of division, all the more to be deplored, since all the contending parties alike appeal to that which one would have thought the most effectual means for putting an end to dissension.

And what is still more to be regretted, instead of diminishing, these divisions increase day by day. Whence does this evil arise? From no other cause than the different or rather contrary interpretations given to the texts severally cited by the parties in question. Where then is the remedy? Obviously, in respecting the true laws of interpretation. These laws are that, when it is desired to know the mind of an author, his expressions should be taken in their obvious and natural sense; that his true meaning should be gathered from the whole context; and the passages which are obscure should be explained by those which are clear and evident. By following these simple rules most of the contentions would cease.

This is what I now propose to show you in reference to the questions of the *origin of ideas* and the *formation of universals;* which will naturally divide our Discourse into two parts. To men of your high intelligence I need not say how important these questions are, and what a source of strife they constitute now-a-days in the arena of Philosophy.

PART I.

ORIGIN OF IDEAS.

4. The true theory on the origin of ideas and on its kindred questions is severally claimed by three contrary schools of thought. One pretends that man has by nature the intuition of the absolute infinite BEING—in a word —of God Himself. The other maintains that man has *innate* the *idea of* BEING ; that is, of being wholly indeterminate, *Ens in communi.* The third, while denying all innate ideas, confines itself to the statement that man has naturally the power of acquiring ideas proportionate to the degree of his intelligence, without, however, telling us in what that power consists.

Respecting the first of these schools, all I have to remark is that its view is contradicted by reason and by experience, and, worse still, is opposed to the principles of faith. Indeed it seems almost identical with the doctrine condemned by the Vatican Council, which has just anathematized those who shall say that that universal indefinite BEING whose various determinations give the genera, the species, and the individuals, is God. The other two schools take their stand on the authority of S. Thomas, each unhesitatingly claiming him for itself. As, however, they are directly opposed to each other, it is evident that S. Thomas cannot be with both, unless we wish to make him contradict himself. But then each side is prepared with numerous quotations from the Angelic Doctor which it is asserted are all clearly in its favour. What must we conclude from this? Surely that one of them misunderstands the teaching of the Holy Doctor. Therefore, in order to ascertain the true meaning of S. Thomas, we must consult his works and explain them in accordance with the rules of fair criticism just laid down. That I may be brief, I shall restrict my observations to two points—that of the *Innate Idea*, and that of the formation of *Universals* from particulars; these points being as it were the two great hinges of the Ideological Question.

5. What does S. Thomas hold respecting Innate Ideas? It must be premised that he has not treated this question *ex professo*, but only touched upon it here and there according as he needed it for developing the theses he had in hand. It is therefore reasonable to expect that his real mind will be most apparent in those places where he has approached the question most nearly. And his words will have to be taken in their obvious and natural sense, unless a logical necessity should compel us to seek for another explanation of their hidden and deep meaning. Nowhere has the Angelic Doctor expressed

himself so clearly on the origin of ideas as in his two
treatises *De Magistro*, and *De Veritate*. In the first article
of the question *De Magistro* he proposes to enquire
"whether God alone, or man also, can instruct and be
"called a teacher," and in the second article: "whether it
may be said that man teaches himself." The first question
he solves thus :—

"The same must be said as regards the acquisition of
"knowledge. Certain seeds of the sciences pre-exist in
"us, that is to say, the first intellectual conceptions,
"which are at once known by the light of the
"acting intellect *(intellectus agens)* through the species
"abstracted from sensible things, be such species complex
"—as the axioms—or be they incomplex—as the nature of
"being, of oneness, and such like—all which are at once
"apprehended by the intellect. From these universal
"principles, as from so many seminal reasons, all the
"other principles are derived. When, therefore,
"the mind starts from these universal cognitions, in
"order actually to know particular things which were
"previously known potentially and as it were in *universali*,
"one is said to acquire knowledge."

Similiter etiam dicendum est de scientiæ acquisitione,
quod præexistunt in nobis quaedam scientiarum semina,
scilicet primae conceptiones intellectus, quae statim
lumine intellectus agentis cognoscuntur per species a
sensibilibus abstractas, sive sint complexa, ut dignitates,
sive incomplexa, sicut ratio entis, et unius, et hujusmodi,
quae statim intellectus apprehendit. Ex istis autem

principiis universalibus omnia principia sequuntur, sicut ex quibusdam rationibus seminalibus. Quando ergo ex istis universalibus cognitionibus mens educitur ut actu cognoscat particularia, quae prius in potentia, et quasi in universali, cognoscebantur, tunc aliquis dicitur scientiam acquirere. *S. Thom. Quaestiones Disputatæ ; De Veritate Quaest. XI. De Magistro, art. 1. Editio Parmae, Vol. IX., p.* 183, *col.* 2.

What say you to this magnificent theory of S. Thomas ? Does it seem to you that this most acute philosopher excludes innate ideas, and not rather that he supposes them as indispensable for the acquisition of all our knowledge ?

But let us follow him : " It must be observed," he writes, "that in natural things something may pre-exist " *potentially* in two ways : 1st, As a power active and " complete, that is, when the intrinsic principle " suffices by itself to produce a perfect act, as we see in " the recovery of a sick man, which is brought about by " his natural vital force ; 2nd, As a passive power, that " is to say, when the intrinsic principle is not sufficient " by itself to produce the act, as for example in the case " of fire kindled in the air ; for this is not the effect of a " force existing in air. It follows from this that, when a " thing pre-exists as a power active and complete, all that " the extrinsic agent does is merely to assist the intrinsic by " supplying it with what it wants for coming forth into the " act. Thus the physician simply ministers to nature, " which is the principal agent, by applying the remedies

" which nature uses as its instruments for producing
" recovery. But when a thing pre-exists only as a
" passive power, the extrinsic agent is the principal
" cause of drawing the act from the power, as we see in
" the air which, being fire in *potentia*, becomes actually
" ignited by the action of the fire."

Sciendum tamen est, quod in naturalibus rebus aliquid
præexistit in potentia dupliciter. Uno modo in potentia
activa completa; quando, scilicet, principium intrinsecum sufficienter potest perducere in actum perfectum,
sicut patet in sanatione: ex virtute enim naturali
quae est in aegro, aeger ad sanitatem perducitur. Alio
modo in potentia passiva; quando, scilicet, principium
intrinsecum non sufficit ad educendum in actum; sicut
patet quando ex aëre fit ignis, hoc enim non potest fieri
per aliquam virtutem in aëre existentem. Quando igitur
præexistit aliquid in potentia activa completa, tunc agens
extrinsecum non agit nisi adjuvando agens intrinsecum
etministrando ei ea quibus possit in actum exire; sicut
medicus in sanatione est minister naturae, quae principaliter operatur confortando naturam, et apponendo
medicinas, quibus velut instrumentis natura utitur ad
sanationem. Quando vero aliquid præexistit in potentia
passiva tantum, tunc agens extrinsecum est quod educit
principaliter de potentia in actum, sicut ignis facit de
aëre, qui est potentia ignis, actu ignem. *S. Thom. De
Magistro, art. I. ib.*

Here one might ask; what have these observations on
active and passive powers to do with our question? I answer,
very much indeed. The Saint wants to give us a palmary
demonstration of the necessity and efficacy of innate
universal principles for the acquisition of knowledge. Let
us hear him. " Knowledge pre-exists in the learner not

" merely as a passive power but also as an active one ;
" otherwise man could never acquire knowledge by
" himself. Even as there are two ways of recovering
" from sickness—one by the power of nature alone, and
" another by the power of nature assisted by medicine—
" so there are two ways of acquiring knowledge. The
" first is when the natural reason learns by itself what it
" knew not before—and this is called *invention*; the second
" is when the natural reason is assisted in learning by
" some external aid—and this is called *discipline.* Be it
" however, observed that in those things which are
" produced concurrently by nature and by art, art acts in
" the same manner and by the same means as natur
" For example, nature cures the affection of frigidity by
" caloric ; so does the physician. Hence the saying : *art*
" *imitates nature.* The same thing happens as regards the
" acquisition of knowledge. Discipline helps the pupil
" to acquire knowledge by the same process which is
" followed in invention. Now the process of invention
" —that is of passing by oneself from the known to the
" unknown—consists in applying the principles which are
" self-evident to some determinate matter ; thence pro-
" ceeding to certain particular conclusions, and from these
" to others. In the same way a person is said to teach
" another in this sense that he sets before him the process
" of reasoning natural to him. This he does by means of
" signs, which the reason of the learner uses as instruments

" for arriving at truths heretofore unknown. Wherefore,
" as the physician is said to cause health to the sick
" through the action of nature, even so one man is
" said to produce knowledge in another through the
" action of the natural reason of the latter. This is
" what is meant by teaching; consequently, a man
" may justly be called the teacher of another. Ac-
" cordingly, Aristotle says that demonstration is a
" syllogism producing knowledge."

Scientia ergo præexistit in addiscente in potentia non
pure passiva, sed activa ; alias homo non posset per se
ipsum acquirere scientiam. Sicut ergo aliquis dupliciter
sanatur, uno modo per operationem naturae tantum, alio
modo a natura cum adminiculo medicinae : ita etiam est
duplex modus acquirendi scientiam ; unus, quando naturalis
ratio per se ipsam devenit in cognitionem ignotorum ; et
hic modus dicitur inventio : alius quando rationi naturali
aliquis exterius adminiculatur, et hic modus dicitur
disciplina.   In his autem quae fiunt a natura et arte,
eodem modo operatur ars, et per eadem media, quibus
et natura.   Sicut enim natura in eo qui ex frigida
causa laborat, calefaciendo induceret sanitatem, ita et
medicus ; unde et ars dicitur imitari naturam. Similiter
etiam contingit in scientiae acquisitione, quod eodem
modo docens alium ad scientiam ignotorum deducit sicuti
aliquis inveniendo deducit se ipsum in cognitionem ignoti.
Processus autem rationis pervenientis ad cognitionem
ignoti in inveniendo est ut principia communia per se nota ·
applicet ad determinatas materias, et inde procedat in
aliquas particulares conclusiones, et ex his in alias ; unde
et secundum hoc unus alium docere dicitur, quod istum
discursum rationis, quem in se facit ratione naturali, alteri
exponit per signa ; et sic ratio naturalis discipuli, per hujusmodi sibi proposita, sicut per quædam instrumenta, pervenit

in cognitionem ignotorum. Sicut ergo medicus dicitur causare sanitatem in infirmo natura operante, ita etiam homo dicitur causare scientiam in alio operatione rationis naturalis illius ; et hoc est docere ; unde unus homo alium docere dicitur, et ejus esse magister. Et secundum hoc dicit Philosophus 1. Posteriorum (com. 5.), quod demonstratio est syllogismus faciens scire. *S. Thom. De Magistro, art* 1. *ib. p.* 183, *col.* 1.

The Angelic Doctor might now have stopped ; for his thesis was conclusively proved. But he would go further in order to make us see that, although a man may teach another, still the principal master is always God Himself.

He continues : " If any one should propose to a learner " things not contained in, or not demonstrable by the " principles which are self-evident, such a one would not " produce knowledge in the learner. He would only " produce opinion, or faith, although even this depends " in some manner on the innate principles. For it is by " virtue of those principles that a man understands that " those things which necessarily follow from them " must be admitted as a certainty ; that those which " are opposed to them must be rejected altogether ; and " that, as to other things, he may either give or withhold " his assent. With regard to the light of reason by which " such principles are manifestly known, it is placed in us " by God by way of a certain similitude of the uncreated " truth. Inasmuch, therefore, as all human knowledge " has its efficacy from that light, it is evident that God " alone teaches interiorly and principally, in the same

'' manner as nature interiorly and principally works the
'' recovery of the sick. Nevertheless man is said with
'' propriety to heal and to teach in the sense aforesaid.''

Si autem aliquis alicui proponat ea quae in principiis
per se notis non includuntur, vel includi non manifestantur ; non faciet in eo scientiam, sed forte opinionem, vel
fidem ; quamvis etiam hoc aliquo modo ex principiis innatis
causetur ; ex ipsis enim principiis per se notis considerat,
quod ea quae ex eis necessario consequuntur, sunt certitudinaliter tenenda ; quae vero eis sunt contraria, totaliter
respuenda ; aliis autem assensum praebere potest, vel non.
Hujusmodi autem rationis lumen, quo principia hujusmodi
sunt nobis nota, est nobis a Deo inditum, quasi quaedam
similitudo increatae veritatis in nobis resultantis. Unde
cum omnis doctrina humana efficaciam habere non possit
nisi ex virtute illius luminis ; constat quod solus Deus est
qui interius et principaliter docet, sicut natura interius
etiam principaliter sanat ; nihilominus tamen et sanare et
docere proprie dicitur modo praedicto. *S. Thom. De
Magistro, art. I. ib., p.* 114., *col.* 1.

6. The identical doctrine is repeated by S. Thomas
in the second article of the same question *De Magistro.*
In reply to the query: '' Whether man may be said to
'' teach himself ?'' he says: '' Certainly, a man may
'' discover many unknown things with the innate light
'' of reason independently of external teaching ; as we see
'' in all those who acquire knowledge by invention. In
'' this way a man produces knowledge to himself. Never-
'' theless, he cannot be strictly called his own instructor
'' and master. . . . For, active instruction imports a
'' perfect actuality of knowledge in the instructor. Hence

" it is necessary that he should possess explicitly and " perfectly the knowledge which he wishes to communicate " to his pupil. But he who acquires knowledge by his " own study, does not start with the full knowledge ready " made, but only with an initial knowledge, that is with " the seminal reasons or the common principles. Conse- " quently he is not entitled to the name of instructor and " master in a strict sense."

Absque dubio aliquis potest per lumen rationis sibi inditum, absque exterioris doctrinae magisterio vel adminiculo, devenire in cognitionem ignotorum multorum ; sicut patet in omni eo qui per inventionem scientiam acquirit ; et sic quodammodo aliquis est sibi ipsi causa sciendi ; non tamen potest dici sui ipsius magister, vel se ipsum docere. . . . . Doctrina autem importat perfectam actionem scientiae in docente vel magistro ; unde oportet quod ille qui docet vel magister est, habeat scientiam quam in alio causat, explicite et perfecte, sicut in addiscente per doctrinam. Quando antem alicui acquiritur scientia per principium intrinsecum, illud quod est causa agens scientiae, non habet scientiam acquirendam, nisi in parte ; scilicet quantum ad rationes seminales scientiae, quae sunt principia communia ; et ideo ex tali causalitate non potest trahi nomen doctoris, vel magistri, proprie loquendo. *S. Thom. De Magistro, art II. ib., p.* 186, *col.* 1.

7. You will admit that this demonstration is truly marvellous and well worthy of the Angel of the Schools. There can be no mistake as to his opinion about the origin of human cognitions, and the great importance he attached to this mode of solving the question. Let us make a few observations on it ; 1st, His reasoning rests

entirely on the distinction between a knowledge which is innate or natural, and a knowledge which is acquired. He teaches clearly that the latter derives all its efficacy and indeed its very possibility from the former; 2nd, his natural and innate knowledge is not a mere potentiality but a something actually existing.

As many persons are of a different opinion, I will quote another text in which the Holy Doctor explains himself so fully as to leave no room for doubt as to his real meaning. In the fourth lesson of his commentary on the third book of Aristotle *On the Soul*, he writes: "No power " passes into action except by something which is in action. " It is so with our power of knowing. However much we " may study or be taught, we can acquire no actual " cognition except by virtue of some actually pre-existing " knowledge, whence that cognition is generated."

Quod in potentia est, non reducitur in actum nisi per aliquod quod est in actu. Et sic etiam de potentia sciente, non fit aliquis sciens actu, inveniendo, neque discendo, nisi per aliquam scientiam præexistentem in actu; quia omnis doctrina et disciplina intellectiva fit ex præexistenti cognitione. *De Anima. l. III., Lect. X. Opera, Ed. Parmæ, vol. xx., p.* 123, *col.* 2.

Is it not evident that, according to S. Thomas, if we deny all innate ideas, that is some kind of knowledge to start from, we annihilate the power of acquiring any knowledge whatever? 3rd, The Angelic Doctor, describes in beautiful order the process of human cognitions. First of all, he says, there is the light of reason placed in man by God, as a resplendent similitude of the first truth. Then come the common and universal principles, which are also self-evident and innate because contained in the light of reason. Yet we do not apprehend them distinctly until the mind by the aid of sensations perceives the terms to which they are applied.

But it may be objected : why then does S. Thomas, after affirming that the principles relating to the *Ens* and the *unum* are innate, say that these principles become known by means of the ideas drawn from sensible things ? Does not this seem to imply that they are innate only in *potentia*, and begin to exist only when the mind abstracts them from the species received through the senses ? Not so, I answer; S. Thomas himself repudiates such interpretation. For, in the sixth lesson on the fourth book of the metaphysics of Aristotle he says: " The first principles are manifested by the " natural light of the *intellectus agens* itself; nor are they " acquired by reasoning, but simply by our becoming " acquainted with their terms. This happens because " from the sensible species we derive memory, from " memory experiment, from experiment the knowledge " of the terms, knowing which terms we apprehend " also the common propositions which are the principles " of the arts and sciences."

Ex ipso lumine naturali intellectus agentis prima principia fiunt cognita, nec acquiruntur per ratiocinationes,
sed solum per hoc quod eorum termini innotescunt. Quod
quidem fit per hoc, quod a sensibilibus accipitur memoria,
et a memoria experimentum, et ab experimento illorum
terminorum cognitio, quibus cognitis cognuscuntur hujusmodi propositiones communes, quae sunt artium et scientiarum principia. *Metaphysic. l. Lect. VI. Opera ib., p.*
353, ccl. 2.

To the first idea of truth in its most universal sense,
and to the common principles therein contained, and
which are developed out of it through the species abstracted from sensible things, succeed all the other
cognitions, which we acquire by applying the innate and
universal principles. This exposition of the nature and
development of the human intelligence accords entirely
with the most rigorous logic and with the data of experience.

8. As a further proof that the above is the genuine
teaching of the Angelical Doctor on innate ideas, I will
adduce another quotation from the question *De Veritate*, art.
IV. His object there was to prove that truth is manifold.
Against this an objection was brought from the doctrine of
S. Augustine, who says that, forasmuch as truth is superior
to our mind, and dwells in God, truth ought to be one,
for God is one. Here is his answer: " What makes the
" soul fit to judge of all things is the first truth. For as the
" innate ideas of things flow into the angelic intelligences

" from the truth of the Divine Mind, and by the light of
" those ideas they know all that they know, so is our mind
" illumined by the truth of the Divine Mind with the truth of
" the first principles, according to which we judge of all
" things. And as we cannot judge except in so far as we
" recognise a similitude with the first truth which is in us,
" even so it is right to say that we judge according to that
" truth." The comparison of man with the angels is very
noteworthy. No one certainly will deny that, according to
S. Thomas, the angels are illumined with innate ideas. But
if so, we must needs concede that, according to him,
man also is possessed of an innate idea ; for he teaches most
clearly that " man receives from the Divine Mind one
" innate idea even as the angels receive many."

Veritas, secundum quam anima de omnibus judicat, est,
verita; prima. Sicut enim a veritate intellectus Divini
effluunt in intellectum angelicum species rerum innatae,
secundum quas omnia cognoscit ; ita a veritate intellectus
Diviniexemplariter procedit in intellectum nostrum veritas
primorum principiorum, secundum quam de omnibus
judicamus. Et quia per eam judicare non possumus nisi
secundum quod est similitudo primae veritatis ; ideo
secundum primam veritatem de omnibus dicimur judicare.
S. Thom. ib., Quaest. I., art. IV., ad 5, p. 11. col. 1.

We must then discard altogether the wonderful treatise
of the Holy Doctor on created intelligences, or accept
this conclusion.

9. Lest the great theory of the Angelical Doctor should
be misunderstood, I am anxious to impress you with the

fact that his admission of the innateness of the common
principles and the seminal causes of knowledge is not
synonymous with the admission of *many* innate ideas,
and of any *special* cognitions supplied by them. For, he
says distinctly that there is but *one innate idea*—that of
truth, or of BEING taken in the most universal sense; and
likewise that this one idea, being entirely indeterminate
gives to man no *special* cognition whatever. His declara-
tions on this head are perfectly clear. In the passages
already quoted from the question *De Magistro*, he declares
that the light of reason is placed in us by God; and
that this light contains indeed the common principles, but
only virtually, or in such a way that, in order that these
principles be developed, the mind must, through sensation,
perceive the terms to which they are applied, and finally, that
all knowledge derives its objective validity from this light
alone. And so in the other passage, when he compares the
human with the angelic intellect, he says that man receives
naturally from God the *similitude*, that is to say the *idea* of
the first truth. Therefore he admits as innate the first idea
only, the most elementary of all, that which is the origin
and the foundation of all the others.

If you ask me "what is this first and innate idea?"
I answer that it is the "idea of BEING;" for in the
first part of the *Summa*, quest. 16th, art. 3rd, he says: "as
" BEING is a convertible term with good, so it is a conver-

" tible term with truth. And as good is BEING in so far as
" it has the relation of appetibility, so truth is BEING in
" so far as it has the relation of intelligibility." ,

Sicut bonum convertitur cum ente, ita et verum.   Sed
tamen sicut bonum addit rationem appetibilis supra ens,
ita et verum comparationem ad intellectum.   *S. 1 hom.
Summa I. Quaest. XVI., art. III.*

And in the 1st art. of the quest. *De Veritate* he writes :
" BEING is that which the intellect conceives as most known
and into which it resolves all its conceptions."

Illud quod primo intellectus concipit quasi notissimum,
et in quo omnes conceptiones resolvit, est ens.   *S. Thom.
Quaest. disputat. Quaest. I.   De Veritate. art. I , p. 6, col. I.*

Consequently, this light, this truth, this innate idea,
being wholly indeterminate and most universal, does not
by itself produce any special cognition in the mind.

The Holy Doctor takes great pains solidly to establish this
view. In the *Summa*, part 1, quest. 55, art 2, he says : " The
" lower intelligent substances, namely the human souls,
" have an intellectual power naturally incomplete.   It be-
" comes gradually completed in proportion as they receive
" the intelligible species from things.   But in the superior
" intelligent substances, *i.e.*, the angels, the intellectual
" power is naturally complete in as much as the intelligible
" species by which they understand everything which they
" can know according to their nature are connatural to them.
" This is seen also by the different manner of the being
" respectively belonging to these two substances.   For

" human souls have a being akin to the body, in as much
" as they are the forms of their bodies. Accordingly, in
" order to attain to their intellectual perfection they
" require the instrumentality of their bodies. Were it
" not so, their union with the bodies would be purposeless.
" On the contrary, the superior intelligences are entirely
" disengaged from bodies—their substances being purely
" immaterial and intellectual; hence they receive their
" intellectual perfection from intelligible species which
" are communicated to them by God together with the
" intellectual nature."

Inferiores substantiæ intellectivae, scilicet animae
humanae, habent potentiam intellectivam non completam
naturaliter ; sed completur in eis successive per hoc quod
accipiunt species intelligibiles a rebus. Potentia vero
intellectiva in substantiis spiritualibus superioribus, id est
in Angelis, naturaliter completa est per species intelligibiles
connaturales, in quantum habent species intelligibiles
connaturales ad omnia intelligenda quae naturaliter cognos-
cere possunt.   Ex hoc etiam ex ipso modo essendi hujusmodi substantiarum apparet.   Substantiæ enim spirituales
inferiores, scilicet animae, habent esse affine corpori,
in quantum sunt corporum formae ; et ideo ex ipso modo
essendi competit eis ut a corporibus, et per corpora suam
perfectionem intelligibilem consequantur ; alioquin, frustra
corporibus unirentur.   Substantiæ vero superiores, id est
Angeli sunt a corporibus totaliter absolutæ, immaterialiter
et in esse intelligibli subsistentes ; et ideo suam perfectionem intelligibilem consequuntur per intelligibilem
effluxum, quo a Deo species rerum cognitarum acceperunt
simul cum intellectuali natura.   *S. Thom. Summa I.
Quaest. LV. art. II.*

To understand fully this splendid passage, we must

observe that according to S. Thomas (as he explains
in the *Summa*, part 1, quest. 85, art. 3rd), the cognition
is incomplete when it apprehends the thing only in
universali, and it is complete when it refers to particular things. Such being the case, it is evident that
by affirming that the human soul has naturally the idea
of BEING in *universali*, he does not attribute to it any
special cognition, because, that idea being most indeterminate, constitutes an intellectual power extremely
incomplete, and therefore utterly insufficient by itself to
give any kind of determination to human knowledge.

10. After these observations we can understand why
S. Thomas, although teaching repeatedly that the human
mind is naturally illumined by truth, or has the intuition
of ideal BEING in *universali*, says in many places that all
knowledge begins by the senses, and that the soul before
acquiring knowledge is like a *tabula rasa*, with nothing
written upon it. By these propositions, far from contra-
dicting himself, he explains the true doctrine under all its
various aspects. In fact, if the most universal innate idea
shows us nothing special, if it can be developed only
through sensation, therefore all determinate knowledge
begins by means of the senses; and therefore before acquiring such knowledge the mind is, as has just been said, a
tabula rasa. But this does not do away with the *innate idea*,
nor with the fact of its being the principle of the human

intelligence, or of its constituting the *formal* part of the human cognitions, the office of the senses being merely to contribute the *material* part. So far as regards *Innate Ideas*.

I now come to my second point—*the Abstraction of Universals*—in which I shall be brief.

PART II.

HOW UNIVERSALS ARE FORMED.

11. Our enquiry will be facilitated by premising three observations.

In the first place :—The Angel of the Schools, while admitting that the idea of indeterminate BEING is innate in man, says also that the universal stands before the human mind prior to all particular cognitions.

In the second place :—This universal, according to S. Thomas, is not an act of the intellect, nor a quality of the intelligent subject, but an *object* seen by the mind. In fact, he declares that "the object of the intellect is " BEING or *common truth*."

Objectum intellectus est ens vel verum commune. *S. Thom. Summa I. Quaest. LV., art. I.*

Therefore, the universal (*i.e.*, ideal BEING or *common truth*) cannot be confounded with the mind which sees it, otherwise, the *object* would be confounded with the *subject*—a contradiction in terms. Besides, in all the places where he teaches that the human intellect knows the truth, the common principles, the moral law, he assumes as an undoubted fact that these universals for such they are, cannot in any way—that is, neither as objects of direct nor of reflex knowledge, be acts of the mind or qualities of it. On no other hypothesis could he be conceived to speak of them (as he always does) as objects present and superior to the mind. To give but one instance. In the third book of his *Summa contra Gentes* he says: "For as much as the law is nothing " but a certain reason and rule of action, it can be " imposed only on beings capable of understanding such " *reason*. But to understand belongs alone to rational " creatures. Therefore, the law ought to be given to " rational creatures only."

Quum lex nihil aliud sit quam quaedam ratio, et regula operandi : illis solum convenit dari legem qui sui operis rationem cognoscunt. Hoc autem convenit solum rationali creaturæ. Soli igitur rationali creaturæ fuit conveniens dari legem. *S. Thom. Contra Gentes, Lib. III. Cap. CXIV.*

I need not say that this rule, to which each singular human action is to be conformed, is an universal. But were we to admit that this universal is an act of the mind itself, the law would be destroyed. For, according to the Holy Doctor, the law stands to the acts of man, and consequently of his mind, in the same relation as a measure stands to the thing measured, or a rule to the thing ruled. Now if the measure and the rule were

identical with the thing measured and ruled, there could
be no such relation; consequently in our supposition there
could be no law. Add to this, that the very idea of law
implies a superiority over those bound by the law. If you
take away this superiority, and remove all distinction
between the law and its subject, the law is gone, unless
indeed you should be prepared to maintain the absurd pro-
position that the subject is at one and the same time
superior and inferior to itself.

In the third place:—According to S. Thomas the
universal is not the substance of real beings; it does not
include their reality at all; it does not exist out of the
mind which contemplates it. That the universal is
not the substance of real beings, nor indeed any substance at all, appears plainly from the 15th lesson on the
7th book of the *Metaphysics of Aristotle*, where our Holy
Doctor writes : " The universal is common to many, that
" is, its nature is to belong to and be predicated of many.
" Now, if the universal were a substance, to what would that
" substance belong ? Evidently, either to all the things in
" which the universal is found, or only to one of them.
" Now it cannot belong to all, for one substance
" cannot be many substances ; nor again can it
" belong exclusively to one, because in that case all the
" other things in which the universal is found would
" be identical with that of which the universal is the

" substance. In other words, an universal is not the
" substance of anything."

Universale est commune multis ; hoc enim dicitur
universale, quod natum est multis inesse et de multis
praedicari. Si ergo universale est substantia, oportet
quod sit substantia omnium quibus inest, aut unius. Non
est autem possibile quod sit substantia omnium ; quia
unum non potest esse substantia pluribus. . . . Sed si
dicatur, quod sit substantia unius eorum quibus inest, oportet
quod omnia sint illud unum, quibus ponitur esse substantia. . . . Relinquitur ergo, quod ex quo universale
non potest esse substantia omnium de quibus dicitur,
nec unius alicujus, quod nullius est substantia. *Metaphysic.*
C. VII. Lect. XIII., p. 498, *col. I.*

This argument is so clear and so unanswerable, that it
seems impossible to take exception to it.

Not less forcible is the way in which S. Thomas
proves that the universal does not include the reality of
the things to which it relates. We find it in *Opusc.* 48th,
on the *Ten Predicaments,* 2nd chap., where he says : " In
" creatures, the essence *(which is an universal)* and the
" actual (or *concrete*) existence differ as two really different
" things. In fact, that which is not contained in the
" essence of a thing differs really from that thing. But
" actual (or *concrete*) existence does not belong to the
" essence of things ; for when we give the definition of
" an object we indicate its entire essence, that is, we
" mention the genus and the difference, but we say nothing
" as to whether the object defined exists actually or not. This
" is evident, for we cannot understand a thing unless we

" apprehend all that belongs to its essence ; whereas it is
" a fact that I understand the thing, a rose for
" instance, even though 1 do not know whether the rose
" subsist or not.   Therefore, actuality or subsistence
" differs really from essence;" or, what comes to the
same, the universal does not in itself include the reality
of beings.

In creaturis esse essentiae et esse actualis existentiae
differunt realiter, ut duae diversae res ; quod sic patet.
Illud enim quod est extra essentiam alicui differt realiter
ab ea. Esse autem actualis existentiae est extra essentiam
rei, nam definitio indicat totam essentiam rei. . . .
Quia in definitione ponitur solum genus et differentia,
et nulla fit mentio utrum res definita esistat vel
non existat.   Apparet hoc manifeste. Nam impossibile
est posse intelligere aliquam rem, non intelligendo ea
quae sunt de essentia ejus.   Tamen constat quod ego
intelligo rosam non intelligendo utrum actu sit vel non.
Ergo actu esse, vel esse actualis existentiae differt realiter
ab essentia. *Opusc. XLIV. (ed. Romana XLVIII.) de*
totius Logicae Aristotelis Summa. Tract. II. cap. II., p. 63.

Lastly, that universals do not exist out of the mind
which has the intuition of them, is most unmistakably
declared by the Saint in numberless places. I shall con-
tent myself with the following. In *Opusc.* 55 he writes :
" Universals as such, do not exist in sensible things ;
" for even their sensibility is in the soul, and no ways in
" them."

Universali ex hoc quod sunt universalia non habent
esse per se in sensibilibus, quia sensibilitas ipsa est in
anima, et nullo modo in rebus. *Opusc. L., p.* 129. *col.* 2.
(ed. Romana LV.)

12. From these remarks I draw three evident conclusions; 1st, Those must be in error who understand S.
Thomas to say that the human intellect abstracts the
universals from sensible things by a power natural to
it, but without being naturally illumined by the *first
universal* which implicitly contains all the others. By
their interpretation, the first operation of the intellect,
which should be drawn from the very fount of all evidence
in order that the light may be diffused over the whole
series of acquired cognitions, is an act done without light
and without sight ; 2nd, To attribute to the Holy Doctor
that the universals exist in the particulars, and that the
universals are simply subjective acts or qualities of the
human mind, is simply to misinterpret him ; 3rd, So also
are those mistaken who quote his authority to prove
that the intellect acts directly on the realities of things,
and on their sensible species, in abstracting the universals from them ; for the universals themselves (of which
man has a natural intuition in the way aforesaid) are the
only means by which the mind can know real things and
judge of them.

13. These erroneous views of the doctrine of S.
Thomas being excluded, it remains to be seen briefly ; 1st,
what operation of the intellect (according to him)
precedes abstraction ; 2nd, how the abstraction itself is
performed ?

As we have seen, he teaches that the knowledge which the human soul has by nature, is incomplete in this sense that the idea of BEING (or the natural light of our intellect) inasmuch as it is wholly indeterminate, gives us no special cognitions. He also says that the soul is united with a body for this very purpose that it may be able to complete its knowledge, in other words, that it may by means of the senses come to. know determinate things. Conformably to this theory, he also declares that man's knowledge is completed by applying the common and self-evident principles, contained in the idea of indeterminate BEING, to determinate matters,. that is to the data of sensation, and hence drawing conclusions, and from these other conclusions again and again.

But how do we apply common principles to determinate matters ? Certainly through *judgment.* For to apply, means to unite one thing to another, and in logic the *predicate* (the universal qualities represented by the common principles) and the *subject* (the sensible impressions caused by the subsistent determinate matters) are united only by a judgment. This judgment is always found in the intellectual perception, by means of which we conclude the subsistence of real things of which we knew nothing before. The necessity of this application of the most universal ideas to the data of sensation in order to acquire knowledge, is stated so expressly and so repeatedly by the Saint, that no one can mistake his mind on the

subject. In quest. x., art. 6, *de mente*, he thus expresses himself: "The sensible forms, that is, the forms abstracted from
" sensible things, cannot act on our mind, except in so
" far as they are rendered immaterial by the light of the
" *intellectus agens*, and thus rendered in some way
" homogeneous with the *possible intellect* whereon they
" act."

Formae sensibiles, vel a sensibilibus abstractae, non
possunt agere in mentem nostram, nisi quatenus per lumen
intellectus agentis immateriales redduntur, et sic efficiuntur
quodammodo homogeneae intellectui possibili in quem
agunt. *De Veritate. Quaest. X. de Mente art. VI. ad I.
Edit. Parmae, .Vol. IX. p.* 164. *col. I.*

And how, I ask, can sensible things be rendered
immaterial and homogeneous with the intellect? Un-
doubtedly by applying the universal idea of BEING to them,
and in that BEING observing the determinations belonging
to each. Thus our intellect apprehends the universal
directly (by intuition), and singular things indirectly,
through having its reflection drawn to them by sensation,
in other words through the primitive judgment; agreeably
to the statement of the Holy Doctor, S. I. quest. 86, art. 1.
It follows from this that, in the process of the human
intelligence, the first operation is the intellectual perception, which applies the universal to the data of sensation.
Then comes abstraction, which draws the universal not
from the real things (in which it does not exist, and upon
which the mind has no power to act), but from the in-

telligible *species* which have been acquired through the intellectual perception. The Holy Doctor says as much : " The *phantasms* are first illumined by the *intellectus* " *agens* (here we have perception), and then again the " same *intellectus agens* abstracts from them the intelligible " species " (here we have abstraction.) (*S. I. quest.* 85, *art.* 1).

Phantasmata et illuminantur ab intellectu agente, et iterum ab eis per virtutem intellectus agentis species intelligibiles abstrahuntur. *S. Thom. Summa.* I. *Quaest. LXXXV. art.* I.

14. Although the mind can know particular things through the universal idea only, nevertheless on first perceiving them its attention is so concentrated on them that it does not reflect on the universal. Now, the attention of the mind to real and determinate things would stop at this stage, were it not for the various *stimuli* which excite the human subject to action. One of the effects of these *stimuli* is to withdraw the attention of the mind from the *subsistence* of the things it has perceived. And this is the first degree of abstraction. It is called *universalization*, for the reason that it leaves before the mind the *intelligible species* by itself alone, that is, not as designating exclusively the individual thing which fell under the senses, but as applicable to all the individuals of the same species. This operation is also expounded by the Angelical Doctor, saying : " When the intellect apprehends

" the intelligible form, or the *quiddity*, as determinate to
"a certain given matter, for example, when it apprehends
" *humanity* as actualized in a particular case—say in this
" flesh, in these bones, etc., then the intellect fixing its
" attention on the concrete, say on this particular man,
" understands the particular, and attributes particularity
" to it. It is not so when the intellect looks at a form
" not as determined to some particular matter; the one
" form being applicable to any number of individuals,
" the intellect attributes universality to it: hence in the
" case alleged we have universal man."

Quando intellectus intelligit praedictam (sc. illud quod
intellectus intelligit de re) formam seu quidditatem ut est
determinata ad hanc materiam, puta humanitatem ut est
in hac materia signata, scilicet in his carnibus et in his
ossibus et hujusmodi; tunc faciendo concretum, puta
hunc hominem, intelligit singulare, et huic attribuit intentionem singularitatis. Si vero dictam formam intelligit
non ut est determinata ad hanc materiam, quia omnis
talis forma de se plurificabilis est ad hanc et ad illam
materiam; habenti talem formam intellectus attribuit
intentionem universalitatis, unde homo est universale.
*Opusc. (Ed. Parmae, XLIV. Ed. Romana XLVIII.) de
totius Logicæ Aristotelis Summa. Tract. I. Cap. II. vol.
XVII. p. 55. col. 2.*

15   Why is universalization the first degree of abstraction ?—Because the only element which the mind drops is
the *subsistence* of the object which it had received.   For the
rest, the *species* of the object remains before the mind in
full, as for instance in the above case, the whole of the

constituents of the man and all his qualities.   But to this
first degree of abstraction succeed innumerable other
degrees, according as the mind withdraws its reflection, not
only from the act of subsistence, as just said, but also from
such among the common qualities found in the thing
represented by the idea as constitute more or less wide
species and genera, until it reaches that most fundamental
and universal of all conceptions without which we could not
think at all—I mean the idea of BEING.   These modes of
abstraction are thus described by the Angelical Doctor in his
treatise on the *Powers of the Soul :* " Now the separations
" resulting from the abstraction of which we speak, do not
" take place in the things themselves, but in the thought
" alone.   For, as in the sensitive powers we find that,
" although certain things be united together in reality,
" nevertheless the sight or any other of the senses can
" perceive some of those things without the other ; even
" so, and for a much greater reason it may happen as
" regards the intellect ; for, although that which dis-
" tinguishes a species and a genus is never realized except
" in an individual, nevertheless the mind may apprehend
" one without apprehending the other.   For example, we
" may apprehend animal in general without thinking of
" man, ox, ass, or any other species of animal ; again
" we may apprehend man without apprehending Socrates
" or Plato ; so also we may apprehend flesh and bones,

" without apprehending this particular flesh, or these par-
" ticular bones."

Ista autem abstractio non est intelligenda secundum
rem, sed secundum rationem. Sicut enim videmus in
potentiis sensitivis, quod licet aliqua sint conjuncta
secunium rem, tamen illorum sic conjunctorum visus vel
alius sensus potest unum apprehendere altero non apprehenso. . . . . ; sic multo fortius potest esse in potentia
intellectiva ; quia licet principia speciei vel generis
nunquam sint nisi in individuis, tamen potest apprehendi
unum non apprehenso altero ; unde potest apprehendi
animal sine homine, asino et aliis speciebus ; et potest
apprehendi homo non apprehenso Socrate vel Platone ; et
caro et ossa . . . . non apprehensis his carnibus et
ossibus. *Opuscul. XL. Cap. VI. Vol. XVII., p.* 31. *col.* 2.
(*Ed. Romana Opusc.XLIII.*)

It is clear, then, that according to S. Thomas, the
intellect, as such, always looks at abstract forms, *i. e.*,
those which are more elevated, without noticing the
inferior ones, except as occasions arise to direct its attention to them.

16. I could add innumerable other texts proving more
and more conclusively that the theory so far explained, on
the origin of human cognitions and on abstractions, is
the one held by the Angel of the Schools. But I must
not tax your patience too much. Besides, the passages
already quoted seem to me quite enough to settle the
matter.

Fully agreeing with those who affirm that the unity

of Catholic teaching, so desirable and necessary, cannot be secured except by taking the great Catholic Tradition for our guide, I have diligently studied the immortal writings of the principal exponent of that tradition; I have searched the places in which he touches most nearly on the arduous questions agitated now-a-days; I have interpreted his expressions in their obvious and natural sense; I have endeavoured to preserve to his testimonies the sense demanded by the logical order of the questions which he was treating; I have sought light from their context, and explained such propositions as seemed to convey an obscure and uncertain sense, by those where the sense was evident. The result has been that I have found that Philosophy of which I have given a rapid sketch in this discourse. I have considered this system and I have seen that it is perfectly free from the grave errors which corrupt modern science to so alarming an extent. In it I have discovered a philosophy which shows the true dignity of man, who, as S. Augustine says, is attached immediately to TRUTH; a philosophy which indicates how man, according to S. Bonaventure, possesses an immutable rule for judging of all mutable things; and last though not least, a philosophy which lays down an indestructible basis for the logical, moral, and social orders. I pray fervently that all men of study may become acquainted with this salutary philosophy, and through it, renouncing all divisions of opinion, and all strife of schools, work together in that unity which is the most valuable characteristic of Truth. Let this philosophy be adopted, and it will be found a most faithful handmaid to theology. We are told in the Gospel that the Word of God enlightens every man that cometh into this world. This is true not less as regards Reason, than as regards Faith. It is the Divine Word Who, while keeping His Essence at present veiled from us, raises our mind by nature to the intuition of *Ideal Truth*. And it is the same Divine Word Who infuses into us the light of Faith, and gives us, in His Supreme Vicar, the Roman Pontiff, an infallible exponent of the Deposit of Faith. Between these two orders of truth, both proceeding from the same Divine source, there can be no collision ; there must be an entire harmony, and the inferior must serve the superior. Therefore, the philosophy of which I have treated under the guidance of the great Angelical Doctor, as it all rests on that truth, by manifesting which the Eternal Word makes men intelligent, so on its part it cannot but prepare men to second the impulses of grace, and to receive with perfect submission from the lips of the Vicar of the Word Incarnate those infallible teachings, which tend to sanctify them in time and to fit them for the blissful fruition, not of the spare rays of Ideal Truth, but of the full Vision of the Truth Subsistent ; not of the Light of Faith to which mysteries still belong, but of the unveiled Contemplation of the Glorious Majesty of God Himself.

☩ PIETRO MARIA FERRE,

Bishop of Casal Monferrato.